WOW!

A Nativity Play for Kids

by
Gwynne Watkins

Beat by Beat Press
www.bbbpress.com

Published by Beat by Beat Press
www.bbbpress.com

WOW!
A Nativity Play for Kids

CAST OF CHARACTERS

ANGEL

NARRATOR

MARY

JOSEPH

SHEPHERDS

WISEPERSON 1

WISEPERSON 2

WISEPERSON 3

CHORUS (includes animals, angels and sheperds)

NOTE: If you'd like to give more kids the opportunities for speaking lines, you can break up the large parts into "Angel 1, Angel 2, Angel 3, etc."

HYMNS

Hymn #1: O Come All Ye Faithful *(Page 2)*

Hymn #2: Away in a Manger *(Page 4)*

Hymn #3: Hark! The Herald Angels Sing *(Page 6)*

Hymn #4: We Three Kings *(Page 7)*

Hymn #5: Joy to the World *(Page 8)*

The lyrics to the Hymns above are included in the back of this book.

PROPS

✓ Donkeys for Mary and Joseph *(Page 4)*

  Suggestion: broomsticks with construction paper donkey head attached to the tip.

✓ "No Vacancy" sign *(Page 4)*

✓ Baby Jesus *(Page 5)*

✓ Star to appear in sky *(Page 6)*

  Suggestion: a star attached to a long broomstick

✓ Gifts of gold, frankincense and myrrh *(Page 7)*

✓ Large cue cards that read: "Wow! What does that mean?" *(Page 8)*

WOW!

A Nativity Play for Kids

WOW!
A Nativity Play for Kids

by
Gwynne Watkins

(ANGEL enters.)

ANGEL
Hail! Hail! Hail!

(NARRATOR enters, in modern-day clothes.)

NARRATOR
Are you trying to get a cab?

ANGEL
No, I'm practicing. I have great news to deliver to everyone on Earth, and I don't want to get it wrong.

NARRATOR
What's the news?

ANGEL
A baby will be born in Bethlehem, and his name will be Jesus Christ. He will be called the Son of God and the Prince of Peace. He will teach people how to love each other, save them from sin and give them life everlasting.

NARRATOR
Didn't that already happen? Like, a long time ago?

ANGEL
Yes, and it's about to happen again! But I need someone to tell the story so that all these people can share in the miracle. Will you help me? *(Pause.)* You do *know* the story, right?

NARRATOR

Well yeah, I think so. The first thing that happens is that the angel appears to Mary.

ANGEL

Hold that thought – I don't want to be late!

(The CHORUS, consisting of animals, angels and shepherds, enters dressed in their costumes. They sing:)

♫ HYMN #1: O COME ALL YE FAITHFUL ♫

(The ANGEL, MARY and the NARRATOR come forward.)

NARRATOR

In a town called Nazareth there lived a woman named Mary. She was engaged to a man named Joseph. God sent the angel to visit her, and at first she was afraid. But the angel said:

ANGEL

Hail, Mary! God is with you!

MARY

Wow! What does that mean?

ANGEL

Well in *your* case, it means that you will have a baby, and he will be Christ the Lord.

MARY

But that's impossible!

ANGEL

Nothing is impossible with God. The baby will be a child of the Holy Spirit. He will be called the Son of God and the Prince of Peace. He will teach people how to love each other, save them from sin and give them life everlasting.

MARY

Does God really love me that much?

ANGEL

God loves all his children, past present and future. But you are special, because you have been chosen to bring his message to Earth.

MARY

If God wants me to do this, then that's what I'll do.

(MARY steps back, JOSEPH comes forward.)

NARRATOR

A few days later, the angel visited Joseph in a dream.

ANGEL

Hail, Joseph! God is with you!

JOSEPH

Wow! What does that mean?

ANGEL

Well in *your* case, it means that your fiancée Mary is going to have a baby. He will be called the Son of God and the Prince of Peace. He will teach people how to love each other, save them from sin and give them life everlasting.

JOSEPH

But that's impossible!

ANGEL

With God, nothing is impossible.

JOSEPH

Are you sure?

ANGEL

Trust me. I'm an angel.

(The ANGEL moves aside. JOSEPH and MARY begin walking.)

NARRATOR

When Mary and Joseph were getting ready to have the baby, they had to take a last-minute trip to Bethlehem. They traveled on a donkey because Mary got tired of nobody offering her a seat on the subway.

ANGEL

I don't think that's in the story.

NARRATOR

Who's telling it, you or me?

(ANGEL shrugs and walks off.)

NARRATOR

By the time they got to Bethlehem, Mary and Joseph were *very* tired.

MARY

Look, a hotel! We can stay there!

(Someone from the CHORUS hangs up a "No Vacancy" sign.)

JOSEPH

Don't worry. I'm sure the angel will appear and tell us what to do.

(Pause. They look around. The Angel does not appear.)

MARY

Let's just stay in that barn.

JOSEPH

Good plan.

(The animals from the CHORUS sing:)

♫ HYMN #2: AWAY IN A MANGER ♫

NARRATOR

Mary had the baby in the barn, because the local hospital didn't take her health insurance.

(The ANGEL walks in, raises a finger to object, then gives up and shrugs.)

NARRATOR (Cont'd)

The animals gathered around the baby, and everyone knew right away how special he was. Meanwhile, the angel appeared to a group of shepherds, who were staying up late to guard their sheep.

(ANGEL and SHEPHERDS come forward.)

ANGEL

Hail Shepherds! God is with you.

SHEPHERDS

Wow! What does that mean?

ANGEL

Well in *your* case, it means that over in Bethlehem, a baby has been born, whose name is Jesus. He will be called the Son of God and the Prince of Peace. He will teach people how to love each other, save them from sin and give them life everlasting.

SHEPHERDS

That's amazing! Where can we find him?

ANGEL

Go that way and look for the baby in the barn. And when you find him, spread the good news that Jesus has been born!

NARRATOR

And suddenly the angel was joined by a whole bunch of angels, and they started singing!

(ANGELS and SHEPHERDS sing:)

♫ HYMN #3: HARK THE HERALD ANGELS SING ♫

(Everyone gathers around Mary and Joseph.)

NARRATOR
And so the shepherds and Mary and Joseph and the angels and all the animals squeezed into the barn to celebrate Jesus' birth. And there was great rejoicing in all the –

ANGEL
Wait! It feels like somebody's missing.

NARRATOR
I don't think you can fit anybody else.

ANGEL
No, I'm sure there was somebody else I was supposed to tell!
(The ANGEL goes into the pews and consults a Bible.)
Oh of course! The three wisepeople! I guess they'll just have to be a little late.

(The WISEPEOPLE come forward.)

NARRATOR
So the Angel went East to a faraway country and appeared to the three wisepeople.

ANGEL
Hail, wisepeople! God is with you!

WISEPEOPLE
Wow! What does that mean?

ANGEL
Well in *your* case, it means that a new star will appear in the sky.
(A CHORUS members holds up a star.)
Follow that star until it stops, and there you will find the baby Jesus. He will be called the Son of God and the Prince of Peace.

ANGEL (Cont'd)
He will teach people how to love each other, save them from sin
and give them life everlasting.

WISEPERSON 1
Let us go now and see this baby!

WISEPERSON 2
Wait! We should bring presents.

WISEPERSON 3
Good idea! Let's bring him gold!

WISEPERSON 1
And frankincense and myrrh!

WISEPERSON 3
What are frankincense and myrrh?

WISEPERSON 1
Things that smell really good!

NARRATOR
So the wisepeople came, and they brought Jesus gifts of gold, and
also frankincense and myrrh, which are things that smell really
good.

(The WISEPEOPLE sing:)

♫ HYMN #4: WE THREE KINGS ♫

NARRATOR
I think that's the end of the story, right?

ANGEL
The end? That's just the beginning! I have to share the good news
with everyone in the world!

NARRATOR
But that's impossible!

ANGEL

With God, nothing is impossible.

NARRATOR

Where do you even start?

ANGEL

We started two thousand years ago in Bethlehem, and we've started again today. Keep telling the story.

NARRATOR

So the angel appeared in [Brooklyn] to [the First Presbyterian Church].

ANGEL

Hail, [First Presbyterian]! God is with you!

(THE CHORUS holds up cue cards:)

CONGREGATION AND CHORUS

Wow! What does that mean?

ANGEL

Well in *your* case, it means that I bring you good news of great joy for all the people. For to you is born this day a savior, who is Christ the Lord. Spread the good news, today and every day – Jesus is born!

♫ HYMN #5: JOY TO THE WORLD ♫

END OF PLAY.

HYMNS

Hymn #1: O Come All Ye Faithful

O Come All Ye Faithful
Joyful and triumphant,
O come ye, O come ye to Bethlehem.
Come and behold Him,
Born the King of Angels;
O come, let us adore Him,
O come, let us adore Him,
O come, let us adore Him,
Christ the Lord.

O Sing, choirs of angels,
Sing in exultation,
Sing all that hear in heaven God's holy word.
Give to our Father glory in the Highest;
O come, let us adore Him,
O come, let us adore Him,
O come, let us adore Him,
Christ the Lord.

All Hail! Lord, we greet Thee,
Born this happy morning,
O Jesus! for evermore be Thy name adored.
Word of the Father, now in flesh appearing;
O come, let us adore Him,
O come, let us adore Him,
O come, let us adore Him,
Christ the Lord.

Hymn #2: Away in a Manger

Away in a manger,
No crib for His bed
The little Lord Jesus
Laid down His sweet head

The stars in the bright sky
Looked down where He lay
The little Lord Jesus
Asleep on the hay

The cattle are lowing
The poor Baby wakes
But little Lord Jesus
No crying He makes

I love Thee, Lord Jesus
Look down from the sky
And stay by my side,
'Til morning is nigh.

Be near me, Lord Jesus,
I ask Thee to stay
Close by me forever
And love me I pray

Bless all the dear children
In Thy tender care
And take us to heaven
To live with Thee there

Hymn #3: Hark the Herald Angels Sing

Hark the herald angels sing
"Glory to the newborn King!
Peace on earth and mercy mild
God and sinners reconciled"
Joyful, all ye nations rise
Join the triumph of the skies
With the angelic host proclaim:
"Christ is born in Bethlehem"
Hark! The herald angels sing
"Glory to the newborn King!"

Christ by highest heav'n adored
Christ the everlasting Lord!
Late in time behold Him come
Offspring of a Virgin's womb
Veiled in flesh the Godhead see
Hail the incarnate Deity
Pleased as man with man to dwell
Jesus, our Emmanuel
Hark! The herald angels sing
"Glory to the newborn King!"

Hail the heav'n-born Prince of Peace!
Hail the Son of Righteousness!
Light and life to all He brings
Ris'n with healing in His wings
Mild He lays His glory by
Born that man no more may die
Born to raise the sons of earth
Born to give them second birth
Hark! The herald angels sing
"Glory to the newborn King!"

Hymn #4: We Three Kings

We three kings of Orient are
Bearing gifts we traverse afar
Field and fountain, moor and mountain
Following yonder star

O Star of wonder, star of night
Star with royal beauty bright
Westward leading, still proceeding
Guide us to thy Perfect Light

Born a King on Bethlehem's plain
Gold I bring to crown Him again
King forever, ceasing never
Over us all to reign

O Star of wonder, star of night
Star with royal beauty bright
Westward leading, still proceeding
Guide us to Thy perfect light

Frankincense to offer have I
Incense owns a Deity nigh
Prayer and praising, all men raising
Worship Him, God most high

O Star of wonder, star of night
Star with royal beauty bright
Westward leading, still proceeding
Guide us to Thy perfect light

Hymn #5: Joy to the World

Joy to the world, the Lord is come!
Let earth receive her King;
Let every heart prepare Him room,
And Heaven and nature sing,
And Heaven and nature sing,
And Heaven, and Heaven, and nature sing.

Joy to the world, the Savior reigns!
Let men their songs employ;
While fields and floods, rocks, hills and plains
Repeat the sounding joy,
Repeat the sounding joy,
Repeat, repeat, the sounding joy.

No more let sins and sorrows grow,
Nor thorns infest the ground;
He comes to make His blessings flow
Far as the curse is found,
Far as the curse is found,
Far as, far as, the curse is found.

He rules the world with truth and grace,
And makes the nations prove
The glories of His righteousness,
And wonders of His love,
And wonders of His love,
And wonders, wonders, of His love.

ABOUT THE AUTHOR

GWYNNE WATKINS is a playwright and lyricist. Her work for children includes the musicals *Tea with Chachaji* (Making Books Sing, NYC) and *Space Pirates!* (Garden Players, Forest Hills NY), the three-play series *In Between Worlds* (New Players, Ridgewood NJ), and *Wow!*, a nativity play for churches. Gwynne is an alumnus of the BMI Lehman Engel Musical Theatre Workshop and a member of the Dramatists Guild. A professional journalist, she lives in New York's Hudson Valley with her husband and son.

WOW! MUSIC KIT

To accompany this play, we created high-quality, original musical arrangements of the five hymns that the kids can perform along with. This "Music Kit" is available as a separate download on our website.

The "Music Kit" includes:

1) Piano-Vocal Sheet Music (PDF): Refreshing contemporary arrangements in keys ideal for young voices.

2) Accompaniment/Backing Tracks (MP3s): Professionally orchestrated tracks that the kids can perform along with, perfectly matching the Piano-Vocal Sheet Music.

3) Reproduction License: A lifetime print and photocopy license for the sheet music (for your organization only).

You can purchase and download this optional Musit Kit on our website: www.bbbpress.com.

ABOUT BEAT BY BEAT PRESS

Beat by Beat Press is the world's fastest growing publisher of original, high-quality musicals for kids, songs for kids and teaching drama resources. The materials are created by a team of professional playwrights and arts educators in New York City and Los Angeles. Since launching in 2011, Beat by Beat shows have been licensed in over 60 countries around the globe.

For more information and over 120 free drama games for kids, visit us at www.bbbpress.com.

Made in the USA
Middletown, DE
19 October 2024

62904074R00015